100 Sunrooms

QUARRY

100 Sunrooms

A Hands-On Design Guide and Sourcebook

David Wilson

GLOUCESTER MASSACHUSETTS

QUARRY BOOKS

First published in the United States of America by:
Quarry Books, an imprint of
Rockport Publishers, Inc.
33 Commercial Street
Gloucester, Massachusetts 01930-5089
Telephone: (978) 282-9590
Fax: (978) 283-2742

Library of Congress Cataloging-in-Publication data available

ISBN 1-59253-027-3

10 9 8 7 6 5 4 3 2 1

Design: Mike Thompson
Cover Image: Courtesy of Canterbury Conservatories (USA)

Printed in China

Contents

Introduction

The use of glass structures to protect plants from the elements dates back to the Roman era. However, sunrooms as we know them originated in Great Britain in the eighteenth century, during the reign of King George III. They were designed as plant houses to conserve specimens brought back from exotic new destinations such as India, China, and the West Indies.

The first conservatories were known as orangeries, as they were used to nurture citrus fruits such as oranges and lemons. Most were solidly built of brick, with large sash windows. In the summer months, plants were moved outside to an adjoining terrace and the orangery was used for entertaining.

In the mid-nineteenth century, advances in glass-making and ironwork enabled the construction of large and technically daring public buildings made entirely of glass. Decimus Burton built the Great Palm House at Kew Gardens in 1844, and Sir Joseph Paxton built the Crystal Palace for London's Great Exhibition of 1851. The concept of grand public conservatories still flourishes in the twenty-first century, given fresh life by structures such as the geodesic domes of the Eden Project in Cornwall, South West England.

The Victorian age was the heyday of the domestic conservatory. New technologies made elaborate glass buildings technically feasible, while the industrial manufacturing of components, using cast rather than wrought iron, made them affordable. Manufacturers produced a dizzying array of styles, many containing romanticized elements of the medieval Gothic style, featuring gables, crestings, finials, and stained glass.

Though still used for the cultivation of plants, conservatories also became a social space; the sunroom was now a fashionable alternative to the drawing-room. Taking tea amidst exotic foliage was a pleasurable new experience available to all. Unsurprisingly, sunrooms also became a favored place for romantic assignations. Ferns and aspidistras were among the most popular plant species, and elaborate heating systems were developed.

Conservatories and sunrooms remained fashionable into the Edwardian era but after the First World War their popularity began to wane. They were considered cold and drafty and expensive to maintain, and innovations such as central heating and fitted carpets made them look outdated. It was not until the last decades of the twentieth century that new materials and construction techniques led to a revival of interest.

Basic types of sunrooms

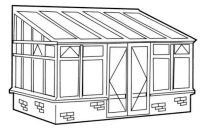

Lean-to The simplest type of sunroom, the lean-to works well on most houses and is a cost-effective option. Lean-tos can be any size, but are often the most suitable choice when space is limited.

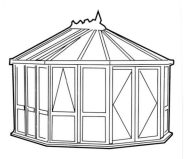

Victorian Perhaps the most popular and stylish of period designs, the Victorian conservatory is characterized by a ridge running at a 90-degree angle from the host wall of the house and a bell-shaped front section. This section is commonly built with either three or five bays, or facets, although there can be more if the structure is particularly large.

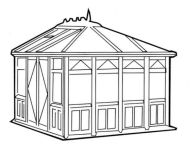

Edwardian The Edwardian-style sunroom also has a ridge running at 90 degrees to the host wall, but the floor plan is square or rectangular instead of bell-shaped. The floor plan also tends to be more flexible.

Gable front This style works well with older houses. The floor plan is again square, but the ridge runs for the whole depth of the roof, giving it a vertical rather than a sloping front section. Normally the glass of the gable is decorated with a pattern such as an arch, a sunburst, or a starburst.

Twin-hip Edwardian A variation on the Edwardian style, this is commonly used where the height of the host wall is limited —as with a one-story house, for example. At the point where the sunroom is attached to the host wall, a box gutter is incorporated into the design, forming an important part of the structure.

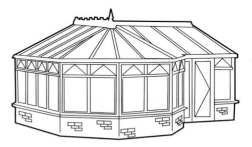

P-shape This style incorporates two sections, a lean-to combined with either a Victorian, Edwardian, or gable-front section. It is more complex and costly to construct, and is best suited to larger houses.

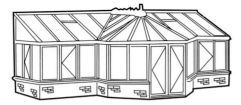

T-shape More complex still, the T-shape conservatory combines a Victorian, Edwardian, or gable-front section with two lean-to sections, one on either side.

Lantern An elaboration on the Victorian blueprint, this design adds height to the conservatory, increasing light levels and giving the option of additional high-level ventilation.

Opposite: A dining room extension is just one of many uses to which a modern sunroom can be put. A sunroom can also be used as a kitchen, a play room, a home office (center), or as a garden room in which to sit and relax (right).
Quantal Conservatory Roofing Systems

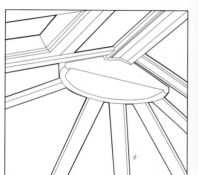

With modern materials and construction methods, conservatories—and sunrooms—are now a practical and affordable option for any homeowner seeking to extend their living space. The construction of a sunroom adds a new dimension to domestic living, providing a "bridge" between indoors and out, as well as adding value to any property.

Sunrooms come in an immense variety of types and styles, from do-it-yourself kits to architect-designed, timber-framed conservatories. They can be used for a wide variety of purposes: as a breakfast room, a kitchen, a dining room, a garden room, a play area, a light and airy home office, or—perhaps most commonly—simply as a space in which to sit and relax and watch the world go by. With the right design, they can be used all year round, even in the depths of winter.

Virtually any house, big or small, can benefit from the addition of a sunroom. The only limit is the homeowner's imagination.

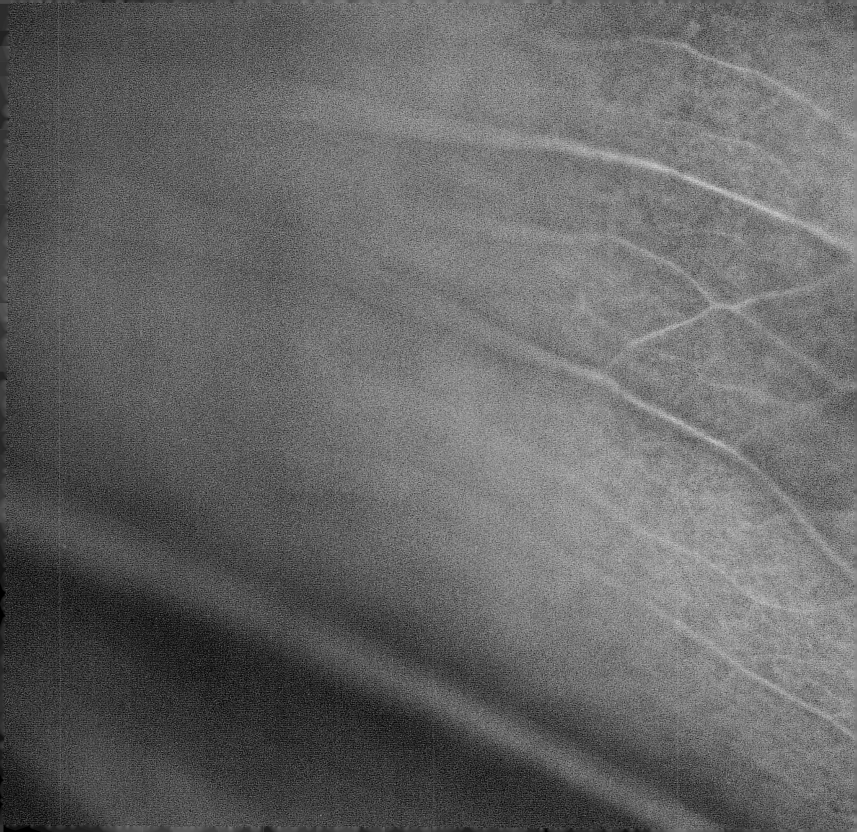

Chapter One

How to Design Your Own Sunroom

Designing your own sunroom

There is a growing trend amongst sunroom companies to use 3D design and visualisation software to assist customers in finalizing their choice of design. With this sophisticated software it is a simple process to produce a design, to demonstrate how options can enhance the appearance, and to show a customer what a new conservatory or sunroom might actually look like attached to their own house.

The DVD tucked inside the back cover of this book gives you the chance to do the very same thing for yourself. The program, Vector Sprint, has been developed by Windowlink, a leading UK conservatory sales software company. It allows you to custom-design your own sunroom, using a range of different components and styles, tailored to fit the dimensions of your own home. The design is displayed in 3D at all stages of the process and, as you select different options, is automatically adjusted and rescaled on-screen. Using your mouse, it can be rotated to view from any angle.

The demonstration version of Vector Sprint on the DVD is designed to work with most standard PCs (unfortunately it won't run on Apple Mac computers). Once you install it on your machine, it will keep running for one year, or twenty sessions.

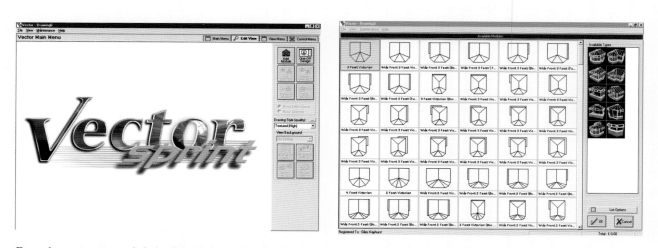

From the main screen, click the Edit View tab. Then click the Add Module button in the top right-hand corner of the screen to reveal the menu of basic floorplans.

Choose your style of conservatory and click OK. As a default, the program is set up to demonstrate a three-facet Victorian sunroom, one of the most popular types.

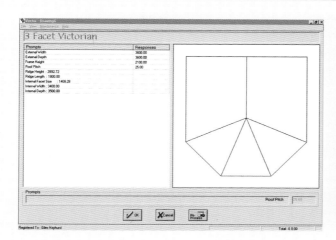
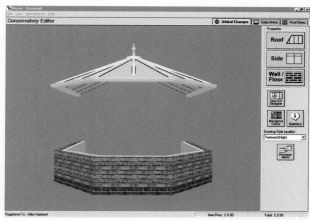

Enter your own dimensions for external width and depth, frame height and roof pitch, pressing Enter or Return each time. When you have confirmed the dimensions, the ridge height, ridge length, and facet sizes will be calculated and displayed on-screen. The program is set up with default dimensions if you simply want to see a demonstration.

Click OK and you have your first view of the conservatory design. To change the angle of view, hold down the left mouse button and slowly move the cursor on-screen.

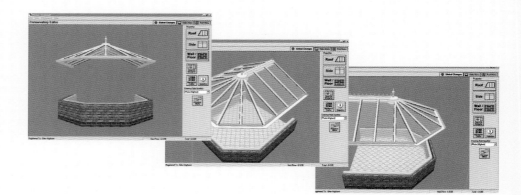

Follow the easy on-screen instructions to install the software. Once this is done, a Vector shortcut icon will appear on your desktop. On the disc you will find a short demonstration: watch this to get an idea of how the program works, and then you are ready to try it for yourself.

The program allows you to choose from a number of popular basic styles (for example, Victorian, Edwardian, lean-to, gable) and adapt them to suit your own tastes. You choose the color of the frame, the type of roof, the style of windows and doors, and a whole range of details, including roof vents, floor tiles, brickwork, and decorative glass panels. As you make your selections, the image is displayed on-screen in full color.

If you have a digital camera or a scanner, you can upload a picture of your house to your PC. The Vector program will automatically superimpose your chosen conservatory design onto the image, so you can see what it will look like in real life. If it doesn't look right, simply go back and start over again.

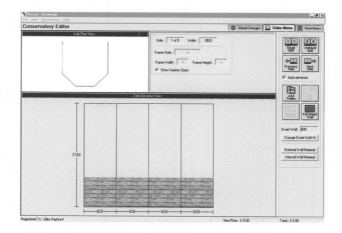

Select the Sides Menu at the top of the screen and click the Add Frame button on the right-hand side of the screen.

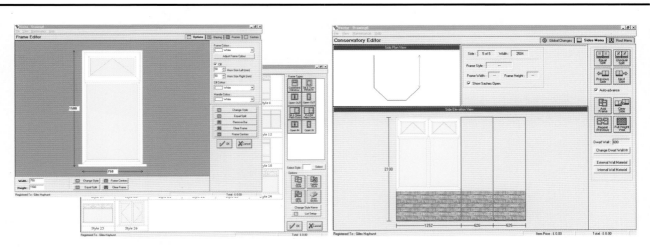

Use your mouse to select a style and click OK.

If you chose the default frame you can simply click the Repeat Previous button to fill in the additional frames quickly, leaving the last two for the doors. Click the Add Frame button again, then the Open Out double door icon.

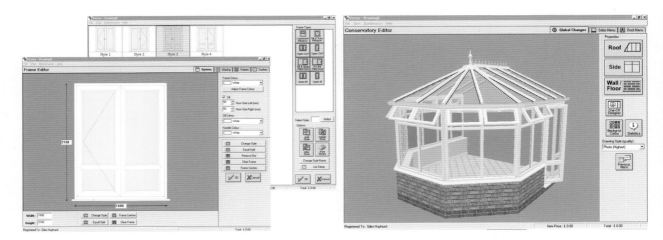

Use your mouse to select a style and click OK.

Click OK again and then the Global Changes tab. You will now be able to see your completed conservatory design. To rotate the design and view it from different angles, hold down the left mouse button and move the cursor slowly around the screen.

Looking at the floorplan

Top tip: When planning your sunroom, sketch
out a plan of the ground floor of your house,
showing the layout of rooms and the position of
doors. This will help you decide on the best way
to integrate the sunroom into the floorplan.

A sunroom is a piece of architecture and should function as an organic part of the structure, not as an awkward add-on or afterthought. When designing a sunroom, the first essential is to look closely at the layout of your house. Any good builder will do this before drawing up plans.

The flow of the rooms is vitally important: The sunroom should complement the interior of the house, and add to its possibilities. Think carefully how you want to use it. Will it be a dining area? If so, it makes sense for it to adjoin the kitchen. If it is to be used as a supplementary living space, it should preferably open off the living room. Doors should be aligned so that it is easy to move from one space to the other.

Even if the area for construction is limited, there are plenty of options available in the orientation of the sunroom that will help it to blend seamlessly into your home.

Architectural quality of sunrooms

Opposite: Together with the frame, glass is the most important architectural component of any conservatory. A high pitched roof creates a wonderful atmosphere of lightness and airiness, while a ceiling fan provides an attractive crowning feature.
Renaissance Conservatories

Far right: Moldings on the frame of the sunroom, and roofing details such as crestings and finials, provide an elegant touch of detail.
Renaissance Conservatories

Right: The choice of glazing panel should reflect the architecture of the main house.
Quantal Conservatory Roofing Systems

Most sunroom designs are based on popular styles of domestic architecture. Classical styles such as Georgian, Victorian, and Edwardian trace their roots back to particular periods of history in the United Kingdom. In the United States the Colonial style is also popular, while many contemporary houses are complemented by modern designs featuring curved glazing panels and aluminium frames.

Within the basic design, however, there is plenty of scope for individuality. Manufacturers offer a huge choice of architectural details, all produced with a high degree of craftsmanship, with which the structure can be embellished. Different styles of glazing pattern, together with various types of colored glass insert, allow the homeowner to stamp their own personal taste on the sunroom.

Ornamental add-ons include roof crestings, finials, brackets, and moldings, all of which help to impart an air of elegance and sophistication. Roof lanterns can be incorporated into larger structures to give a truly spectacular architectural quality.

Left: This large conservatory provides a dramatic architectural feature. The roof gable has been designed to echo the shape of the window gables of the house, creating unity between the old structure and the new.
Amdega Ltd

Opposite: This Gothic-style porch conservatory was built as an extension to a London townhouse. Running off the kitchen, it doubles as a dining room and a garden room, optimising the use of space in a relatively small area. Its high pitched roof allows the maximum amount of light to penetrate the interior.
Amdega Ltd

It is very important that the style of the sunroom matches the style of the house to which it is attached, especially if the house is built in a period style. This can be achieved by incorporating elements that echo its original features, such as window gables, eaves, and decorative moldings.

Sunrooms should blend into the existing architecture of the house to extend the available living area. In an urban setting, where space is often limited, a small sunroom built onto the back of a townhouse can open up new possibilities for dining and entertaining. In a rural or suburban location, where more space is available, there is scope for a larger conservatory providing a transitional space between house and garden.

Whatever the setting, the most successful designs have an architectural quality that makes the sunroom appear an original part of the house.

The importance of design

Opposite: When a sunroom is properly integrated with the design of a property, it becomes a valuable link to the outside world.
Hampton Conservatories

Right: This welded aluminium sunroom in Cincinnati, Ohio, was originally a show model for a home and garden show. The owner, an interior decorator, added it to her home as a dining area adjacent to a small kitchen.

She repeated the blue accents in the lantern glass in the surface of the interior kneewall.
British Conservatories Inc

Above: This large pool room extension, built onto a house in Pennsylvania, features a number of special design features, including French doors, concealed downspouts, custom moldings, and a fan gable with a half-round starburst design.
British Conservatories Inc

Each sunroom has its own character, which reflects the taste and imagination of its owner. Whatever the style of the sunroom, however, and wherever its location—in the town, in the country, or in the suburbs—design is all-important, at every stage of the planning and construction process.

There are a number of issues to consider. First of all comes location. Where can the sunroom be built, and how will it connect with the existing rooms of the house? Then comes size. A sunroom structure should be in proportion to the rest of the house, and should complement it, not dominate it. Next is the choice of style and shape, which will be dictated to a large extent by the design of the house itself. The choice of glazing styles and architectural ornamentation offers an almost infinite number of possibilities. Just as important is the interior design, including the color scheme and the choice of furniture, fabrics, and blinds.

Top tip: As much as possible, architectural details should reflect the style of your house. Take a close look at windows, eaves, gables, and roof ridges and try to select a sunroom style that will match.

Sunroom designers strive to make the best possible use of the space available. They often work backwards, starting with the footprint into which the structure must fit, and then selecting components whose proportions and materials are in harmony with the main house. At the same time, they aim to make the sunroom sympathetic to its outside surroundings, which may involve a certain amount of landscaping.

Whatever type of house you live in, and however small the space you have available, a sunroom can be constructed to suit it. Thoughtfully designed for its environment, a conservatory adds pleasure to life and also becomes an asset that enhances the property's architecture and value.

When planning a new sunroom, try to visualise from the start how the finished product will look, and bear in mind at all times the essential role of good design. Properly applied, this will help to create a structure that works just as well aesthetically as it does practically.

Chapter Two

Simple Sunrooms: Lean-tos, Bump-outs, Solariums, and DIY Kits

Lean-tos

Opposite: A lean-to sunroom with a porch extension provided a "bridge" between two traditional stone farm buildings.
Amdega Ltd

Right: The sunroom provides an alternative dining area for summer evenings, with double doors and steps leading up to the garden.
Amdega Ltd

Top tip: A sunroom should look like an integral part of the house, and not just an add-on. From the very start, try to visualize the design of the extension as a whole, from its overall size and shape down to the details of the interior furnishings.

Lean-tos are the simplest types of sunroom extension, but they can be adapted in all manner of ingenious and creative ways. In the example shown here, the designers were faced with the challenge of linking two traditional, Grade II-listed stone buildings on a farm in the West of England.

The L-shaped space between the house and the adjoining barn conversion was south-facing and sunny, but also open to drafts. The solution was a rectilinear lean-to sunroom built between the two buildings, which effectively combined them into one extended living space. A gabled porch entrance extended the space further into the garden, while an awkward gap on the other side was filled by a glazed door and roof.

A mellow green paint finish for the frame and an assortment of rustic wooden furniture helped to create a light and spacious garden room which blends in well with the overall style of the house.

Left: This porch-type sunroom fits snugly into the corner space created by the angle of the main building. The pots outside help provide a transition to the garden.
Quantal Conservatory Roofing Systems

Opposite: A simple lean-to structure, here attached to a bungalow, opens up the house and provides an ideal spot in which to sit and appreciate the surrounding garden.
K2 Conservatory Roof Systems

Below: Even a small sunroom can add an extra dimension to a house, creating a new living area or an outdoor dining room.
Quantal Conservatory Roofing Systems

Even within the confines of a small suburban garden, a sunroom can add a sense of space and lightness to a house. A simple lean-to structure can be used to extend a living room or dining area and provide a "corridor" to the garden. Filling the conservatory with plants will help to create a sense of continuity with the outdoors.

The lean-to is a popular choice for many homeowners. It is relatively simple to construct and maintain, which means that costs are lower than for some more complex styles of sunrooms. Its flexible configuration means it can be adapted to fit any space, however small it may be. Even the smallest of lean-tos, however, adds a whole new dimension to the house.

Their uses are varied—the most popular choices are sitting rooms, dining rooms, or a garden room that combines the lightness and space of outdoors with the comfort and climate control of indoors.

It was once the case that conservatories were enjoyed as garden rooms in the warm summer months, but scarcely used in the chilly days of winter. This is certainly not true of today's conservatories. Modern sunrooms are designed to be used all year round, summer and winter, spring and fall.

Each season has different requirements. In summer ventilation is key, with windows and roof lights that can be opened, and the option of sun blinds for shade. In spring and fall the idea is to make the most of any sunshine there may be, but also to block out drafts and protect plants against unseasonably late or early frosts. In winter, quality double glazing, combined with a central heating system, can make the sunroom a warm and inviting place, even on the coldest and dreariest of days.

In parts of the United States, snow loading is an important consideration and regulations stipulate that sunroom construction should be sturdy enough to withstand substantial snowfall.

The materials used in sunroom construction depend on the location, the type of sunroom selected, and the homeowner's budget. Traditional sunrooms featuring hardwood timber frames tend to be quite costly, especially as they are often custom-designed. However, simple designs featuring curved wooden eaves are available from a number of suppliers, particularly in the United States.

For simple sunrooms, a popular choice is ultraviolet-resistant polyvinyl chlorate, or PVC-U, a plastic material that looks stylish, and is hard-wearing and easy to maintain. Aluminium frames are also popular, especially when extra strength is required; frequently they are covered with PVC-U cladding. There are numerous types of glass available for the side walls.

Many come as sealed double-glazing units, and some are specially toughened or tinted.

Roofs can be made of glass, or in some cases a specially toughened polycarbonate material. Not all roofs are see-through. Many sunrooms, particularly in the United States, have solid slate or shingle roofs designed to complement the roofing of the main house.

Opposite: This sunroom has a glass roof with a curved eave, designed to blur the line between sky and landscape.
Four Seasons Sunrooms

Right: A sunroom of this type can be used all year round, providing a cool oasis in the summer and a cosy retreat in the winter months.
Four Seasons Sunrooms

Top tip: Hardwood timber is the most traditional, and to some minds the most elegant, material for sunroom frames. For many homeowners, however, aluminium or PVC-U may be a more practical choice. Both materials are economical, hardwearing, and easy to maintain.

The orientation of the sunroom is a factor to consider at the initial design stage, and to some extent will influence the way it is used. Normally the goal is to maximize the amount of sunlight it receives, but in some cases this may be constrained by the layout of the house, the space available for construction, and the surroundings, including tall trees or neighboring buildings.

A north-facing sunroom receives the least sunlight. This means that blinds are less likely to be needed, although heating becomes more of an issue. A south-facing sunroom can get very hot in summer, and needs plenty of opening windows and roof vents to ensure air circulation. Blinds and tinted glass can help to protect against strong sun, and air-conditioning may also be worth considering.

A sunroom that faces east gets the sun in the morning and so makes a good breakfast room. A west-facing one gets most sun in the afternoon and early evening, and so is more suited to relaxing at the end of the day.

Solariums and bump-outs

Right: This spectacular design features soaring wooden beams and large sections of glass, allowing its owners to dine in comfort under the stars. *Four Seasons Sunrooms*

Center: With the addition of a sunroom extension, a dark attic space has been transformed into a bright, light-filled home office. *Four Seasons Sunrooms*

Opposite: This elegant and airy dining area has been created by opening up the former exterior wall to let the light flood in. Sliding doors lead out to a balcony area. *Four Seasons Sunrooms*

A sunroom is not always necessarily a separate structure. Some of the simplest are extensions of internal rooms. Where there is no room for a free-standing sunroom, a "bump-out" or "enclosure" can be a very effective means of creating extra space, opening up gloomy interiors, and letting the light flood in.

Bump-outs can be adapted to suit any part of the house. They do not have to be at ground level, and do not necessarily need doors that open to the outside world. Sunrooms on an upper story will benefit from opening doors if there is a balcony or decking area outside; on the other hand, outside access is not normally required for an attic bump-out that is built into the roof of the house.

Sometimes the word "solarium" is used to describe either a bump-out or a sunroom in general. This is not a precisely defined term, but merely denotes any space in which one can sit and enjoy the sun's rays.

Do-it-yourself

Opposite: Removable glazing panels mean that the sunroom remains snug in the winter but can be opened up to the fresh air in the summer.
Sunporch.com

Below: Internally, there is plenty of room for sun loungers, tables, or even a home spa tub. A self-assembled sunroom is as flexible a space as any other.
Sunporch.com

Right: The self-assembly sunroom supplied by this US manufacturer is straightforward to build and can be attached to any type of house.
Sunporch.com

If you enjoy DIY, it is perfectly feasible to build your own sunroom. Many companies supply complete sunrooms in the form of do-it-yourself kits. These are relatively simple to assemble, given some basic skills and a degree of patience. They provide a substantially cheaper option than hiring a builder and, when completed, give a real sense of satisfaction.

With self-build, you become in effect your own contractor and can manage the project to suit the time you have available. If certain jobs don't appeal to you—such as digging the foundation, for instance—you can always hire a builder to do these for you.

You do need a degree of confidence to tackle a project of this sort on your own, and it may be a good idea to enlist the help of a friend or neighbor. Not only are an extra pair of hands useful in carrying out construction tasks; an extra pair of eyes will reduce the risk of making mistakes and having to go back and start over again.

Chapter Three

Period Style: Georgian and Regency

Georgian and Regency

The three most popular period styles for sunrooms are Georgian/Regency, Victorian, and Edwardian. Each has its own characteristics, derived from the styles of architecture that prevailed in those periods of British history. However, definitions of period style are sometimes rather hazy, and can vary from manufacturer to manufacturer.

The Georgian style of architecture developed during the reign of King George III, which lasted from 1760 to 1820. Inspired by classical Greece and Rome, it was characterized by clean, straight lines, large sash windows, and expanses of stucco plasterwork. Many grand Georgian houses still survive today; the best examples include the sweeping London terraces designed by architect and town planner John Nash.

George's son, a patron of the arts, became Prince Regent in 1811 and succeeded him as King George IV in 1820. The style of architecture associated with his reign is rather more exuberant. Examples include the oriental fantasy of the Brighton Pavilion.

Opposite: This Georgian-style sunroom in Ann Arbor, Michigan incorporates a number of traditional elements and combines a rectangular, gabled section with a lean-to.
Town and Country Conservatories

Left: This stylish structure has stone balustrades and decorative ironwork based on Georgian prototypes, and windows that echo the design of the Georgian sash window.
British Conservatories Inc

The Georgian style of conservatory grew out of the classical architecture that was employed for orangeries. These were used to conserve delicate plants, particularly fruiting citrus trees, collected by travelers in exotic climates. They were typically brick-built, and sometimes clad in stone, with solid roofs, but also had floor-length sash windows that could be opened up wide in summer.

As glazing technology improved, glass roofs were introduced. These made it easier to grow plants all year round, and also added to the orangery's social possibilities. They were the perfect place for tea and supper parties, while the larger ones were sometimes even used as ballrooms. Many of these sturdily built early orangeries still survive today.

Modern Georgian-style conservatories are still generously proportioned. Typically, they are rectangular in shape, with a glazed gable end embellished with a pattern such as a sunburst. The gable section may be attached directly to the house, or it may be combined with a lean-to section. Glazing patterns are frequently modeled on the Georgian sash window.

Manufacturers commissioned to build sunrooms for period Georgian houses face different constraints, and possibilities, depending on whether the house is located in the town or in the country. The example shown here, built onto a terraced Georgian townhouse in Shepherd's Bush, London, is a typical solution for an urban setting where space is limited.

In this kind of location, the sunroom need not necessarily be built at ground level. Here, it is supported by a new extension added to the lower ground floor (which is used largely as a cellar). Exterior steps connect the garden with the main living space, situated on the upper ground floor. A door at the end of the balcony lets light and warmth into an adjoining study, and also provides an additional route into the living room.

The lantern roof, inspired by the Georgian architecture of the house, adds height to the structure and allows the maximum amount of light to enter all year round. The conservatory has a perfect view of the garden below and is used by its owners primarily as a garden room.

Opposite: This elevated sunroom, attached to a colonial-style house in Taylors, South Carolina, is built on a masonry foundation and encircled with a deck landing which leads down to a garden and swimming area. Its gable elevation features a half-round fanlight.
British Conservatories Inc

Above and right: These two British examples demonstrate a few of the choices available in glazing panels, gable design, and decorative crestings and moldings. In both, however, the materials used for the knee wall closely match the style of the house.
Quantal Conservatory Roofing Systems

Georgian designs can be adapted to suit a whole range of domestic settings. As with any sunroom, they must take account of local styles of architecture and building materials. For example, if the sunroom incorporates a knee (or dwarf) wall, this should match the type of material in which the main house is constructed.

In the detail, however, the variations are limitless. In some cases glazing panels are plain, and limited to three or four sections, with a small number of opening windows. Others are divided up into a grid of tiny panes, echoing the more ornate styles of Georgian sash window, and there may be openable casements all round.

The gable end can be made entirely of glass, or it can be partly filled in with wood, PVC-U, or aluminium. The decorative pattern it contains can follow a variety of configurations, as elaborate as you like. Sunbursts and starbursts are the most popular patterns, but in some cases a sealed unit featuring a stained-glass pattern is inserted instead.

Top tip: Don't worry if space is limited. Most designs can be adapted to fit the space available, and even a small sunroom can make a remarkable difference to your living area.

A Georgian-style sunroom can look just as good on a modest dwelling in town as on a grand country house. Here we see two variations on a theme: a grand sunroom in the countryside, with multiple facets and two sets of double doors, and a small porch-style structure built onto the back of a townhouse.

In each case the basic design has been adapted to fit the space available, with the result that both are admirably suited to their environment. The larger structure makes use of a former patio area to extend an already spacious interior into the garden beyond. It has an elaborate timber frame and a rich tracery of window and roof panels. The decoration is ornate, with crestings and finials on the roof ridges and ornamental pilaster moldings incorporated into the frame.

The smaller urban sunroom is much plainer, but performs the same function as its country cousin. It blends in well with the architecture of the house, and adds a new dimension to the domestic living space.

Opposite: Double doors lead out onto a small raised patio area, while side-opening windows and a high-level roof vent keep this sunroom cool in summer.
British Conservatories Inc

Right: This conservatory has an interior gable shelf that can be used to display plant pots or ornaments, and its doors leads out into a lovingly landscaped back yard.
British Conservatories Inc

Sunrooms built in the Georgian or Regency style have a long history on both sides of the Atlantic. They are frequently found on houses in Great Britain, where the style originated, but they are also very popular in the United States, where they work well with colonial-style homes.

The example pictured opposite is built onto a colonial ranch-style house set within Montgomery State National Park in Pennsylvania. It features welded aluminium construction, and has a pitched roof with a starburst gable decoration and a high level vent. Surrounded by trees and with distant views of mountains, it adjoins an entertainment room inside the house.

Its owners use it primarily as a sitting area and reading room.

Also located in Pennsylvania, the 16x16 ft gable roof conservatory above was created for a keen gardener who uses it mainly for overwintering delicate plants. Its exterior surfaces are of polyurethane-coated aluminium and its sashes are constructed of vinyl, which means it requires little maintenance.

Left: This English conservatory was deliberately designed to mirror the architecture of the house, with matching stone basework and glazing inspired by the Georgian sash windows. *Amdega Ltd*

Designed for a period home in North Yorkshire, the generous proportions and glazing style of this rectangular, gable-ended conservatory were inspired by the classical Georgian architecture of the house. The owners wanted to link their living space more closely with the garden.

The stone foundation walls match the façade of the house, while the glazing echoes the style of the elegant Georgian sash windows. The fanlight set in the gable end of the roof provides an attractive feature, while the ridge cresting and carved finial, and the dentil molding around the top of the frame, add ornamental touches. The same style of paving slab was used for the interior as for the terrace outside, creating continuity between indoors and out. The conservatory contains a luxuriant climbing plant, giving the interior an exotic feel. The result is a light and airy extension that can be used all year round.

Chapter Four

Period Style: Victorian

Victorian style

Opposite: This sunroom in Northfield, Illinois displays the traditional Victorian shape, with a bay end and crested roof ridge, though the wishbone glazing pattern is modeled on the style of the neo-Georgian house.
Town and Country Conservatories

Right: The interior provides a cool and tranquil haven, shaded by roof blinds. The tiled floor and wrought-iron furniture make it feel like an extension of the garden.
Town and Country Conservatories

The Victorian style is based on the architecture that evolved during the long reign of Queen Victoria, which stretched from 1837 to 1901. The Victorian age was a prosperous and forward-looking one, a time of rapid technological advance, and innovation in industry, science, and the arts.

Much of its architecture, however, harked back to the past. Brick was the favorite building material, but a romantic revival of the medieval Gothic style saw buildings adorned with arches, pinnacles, buttresses, and intricate stone fretwork inspired by the fan-vaulted ceilings of Europe's medieval cathedrals.

New techniques in the production of glass and iron made possible the construction of vast public buildings made of glass, such as the Great Palm House at Kew and Paxton's Crystal Palace. Glass roofs were also used for shopping arcades, museums, and railway stations and, increasingly, for domestic conservatories. The Gothic style was carried over into these structures and the decorative use of braces, brackets, crestings, fanlights, finials, floor grilles, and gables became ever more elaborate as the nineteenth century progressed.

Relatively few original Victorian conservatories have survived to the present day. Iron is vulnerable to rust and frost damage, and needs constant repainting, and most of the early structures were allowed to fall into disrepair. The Victorian style, however, still flourishes, reinterpreted using modern materials such aluminium, PVC-U, and sustainable hardwood from carefully managed forests.

The style is characterized by a roof ridge running at a 90-degree angle to the main house, and a bell-shaped front section made up of a number of bays, or facets. Three or five facets is the most usual number, though there can be more if the structure is particularly large.

The roof is normally decorated with cresting and finials inspired by Victorian Gothic designs. Glazing may be plain, though may also be decorated with leaded panels of colored glass. As with other period styles, the definition of Victorian can sometimes be a little hazy. Manufacturers interpret the style in slightly different ways, and may combine it with elements more typical of other periods.

Top tip: When washing down your sunroom,
use only a soap and water solution. Avoid
solvent-based or abrasive cleaning agents,
as these may damage the surfaces. To remove
stubborn marks, use a non-abrasive proprietary
cleaner suitable for plastics, with a soft cloth.

The Victorian style is an extremely popular one, and very adaptable too. It works well in a wide variety of locations, with many different styles of domestic architecture, and can be adapted to fit the space available, whether a large garden, a small patio area, or a cramped cornerfill site.

Two popular variations on the style are the P-shape and T-shape Victorian. Suitable for larger sites, the P-shape combines a conventional Victorian section with a lean-to extending along the wall of the house, which greatly increases the sunroom's internal floor area. The T-shape is larger still, featuring two lean-to sections adjoining the central portion, one on either side.

For Victorian-style sunrooms with frames made of aluminium or PVC-U, the most popular choice of color is a traditional crisp white. However, darker shades are also available, such as mahogany and rosewood. Timber-framed sunrooms can be painted any color, though muted tones, such as soft greys and greens, usually work best.

Left: A classic Victorian design, which extends the living area into a spacious garden, creating a warm and homey focus for family life. *Renaissance Conservatories*

Opposite: This Victorian-style sunroom, which features hardwood construction and a roof lantern, is an ideal place in which to enjoy the colors of fall. *Renaissance Conservatories*

When selecting a sunroom supplier, the number of companies you need to approach depends on your requirements. If you have a difficult site, or want a bespoke hardwood conservatory to fit with a listed building, there will be a relatively limited number of manufacturers that can meet your needs. For basic PVC-U or aluminium conservatories, the choice of supplier is much wider.

If your project is particularly large or complex, it may be worth paying an architect or draftsperson to draw up some plans for you. This will give you an impartial idea of what is possible and practical, and may save time and money when it comes to dealing with potential suppliers.

It is also a good idea to allow a contingency fund–say around 10 percent of the total quoted price–to meet any additional costs during the course of construction. You may decide to upgrade certain specifications, for example, or there may be a need for unforeseen building work or landscaping. When the work is complete, don't forget to inform your home insurance company about the new extension.

The Victorian and Edwardian owners of conservatories rarely gave much thought to maintenance—after all, they had gardeners and domestic servants to take care of it for them. Few of us have that luxury today. However, modern sunrooms are designed to be as low-maintenance as possible—indeed, aluminium and PVC-U types virtually take care of themselves.

Manufacturers recommend that every few months you wash frames, glass, and roof panels, using soapy water, to get rid of grime and atmospheric deposits. When you do this, be sure to remove rings from your fingers to avoid scratching the surfaces, and don't press too hard on leaded lights, as this may dislodge the colored glass panels.

Check that drainage vents are clear of leaves and other debris, and that weather seals around doors and windows are safely in place. From time to time, you should oil the hinges and locks of doors and windows.

Timber-framed sunrooms need a little more attention, but even here maintenance is not the chore it once was. Count on having to repaint or varnish the exterior once every three to five years.

Opposite: This 18×14 ft octagonal conservatory, built in solid mahogany, was part of a renovation plan for a period Victorian home in Hingham, Massachusetts. It doubles as a dining room and a cozy lounge for entertaining.
British Conservatories Inc

Right: The roof structure of this single-story home was extended to make the new sunroom an integral part of the building.
*Tull and Darch/
Regal Conservatories of Utah*

Ventilation and heating requirements fluctuate according to the seasons. You should design your sunroom to be comfortable throughout the year, depending on how you plan to use it. Important factors to consider include its orientation—whether it faces north, south, east, or west—and whether neighboring buildings or overhanging trees block out any light.

Color schemes have a dramatic effect on the feel of a sunroom. A cool, north-facing space can be warmed up by vibrant colors such as terracotta, red, and orange. Sunnier, south-facing sunrooms benefit from paler shades, such as light blues and pale yellows.

Blinds offer protection from the glare of the sun, and also a degree of privacy—important if you are overlooked by neighbors. In hot climates, insect screens may be a blessing in summer.

Candles create a special atmosphere at night, but day-time heat can cause them to bend or melt. Don't neglect shading and ventilation when you go away on vacation—you may return to a sunroom full of dead plants.

Left: Nestled among the trees, this elegant Victorian conservatory adds the old-world feel of an English garden to a period brick-built house.
Four Seasons Sunrooms

Opposite: At night, a sunroom is a magical place for entertaining or simply for sitting and admiring the stars.
*Tull and Darch/
Wendland Roof Solutions*

Sunrooms are transformed at night. The structure takes on an entirely new dimension, whether open to the breeze on a summer evening or snugly insulated against the elements in the winter months. Dining under the stars is a novel and exhilarating experience. Some stargazers go further, installing a telescope to convert the room into a home observatory.

Day or night, security is an important issue to consider. Sunrooms are generally tucked away at the back of the house, but for the opportunist thief they may offer a tempting route into the home. Make sure that windows, doors, and any accessible air vents are fitted with good-quality locks and bolts, and secure them when you go out.

Lockable doors separating the sunroom from the main house create an extra cordon of security, and most domestic alarm systems allow sunrooms to be incorporated into the circuit. Nevertheless, take care to keep valuable items out of sight—if you use your sunroom as a home office, for example, don't leave your laptop computer unattended on the table.

Opposite: A roof lantern adds extra height to a sunroom, allowing light to flood in and making the structure feel more spacious. *Ultraframe (UK) Ltd*

Right: The panels of the lantern section are sometimes plain, but many are embellished with leaded sections or colored glass designs. *British Conservatories Inc*

A roof lantern is an impressive addition to any large Victorian-style sunroom. Forming a superstructure to the main roof, it dramatically increases the impression of interior space. It may incorporate high-level roof vents that encourage air circulation, helping to keep the sunroom cool on hot days.

Most feature a *clerestory* (or clear story) that provides a perfect setting for decorative glazing patterns. These may be part of the glazing panels themselves or formed by leaded lights—sections of colored glass held in place by lead strips. Typical designs include diamond and lozenge shapes, although others feature flowers or even birds. The play of sunlight through colored glass is a most attractive feature.

The glass used in the main structure of the sunroom wall is likely to be tempered or laminated, for extra strength and safety. Safety glass is hard to break, though not impossible. When hit with force, it is likely to crack rather than shatter into pieces.

Chapter Five

Period Style: Edwardian

Edwardian style

Left: The style is generally very flexible in its configuration and can be adapted to fit in with most styles of domestic architecture. *Amdega Ltd*

Opposite: Edwardian-style conservatories are rectangular in shape and are characterized by a triangular-section hipped roof. *Amdega Ltd*

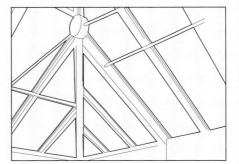

The reign of King Edward VII extended from the death of Queen Victoria in 1901 to his own demise in 1910. It was a langorous era of tea parties and romantic intrigue, when conservatories were built onto smaller houses by enthusiastic middle-class families.

The Edwardian style was a refinement of Victorian taste. The conservatory footprint became rectangular, though many of the embellishments, such as crestings and finials, were retained. The fashion was for a simple hipped roof design (characterized by a triangular section coming to a point where it meets the apex), which blended in well with most styles of architecture.

Edward was succeeded by another George, and then the First World War changed the world forever. The jazz age of the 1920s and 1930s embraced modernity, and drafty conservatories were considered an anachronism in an age of steel and chrome. Gradually they fell out of favor, and many of the old ones were demolished or simply allowed to crumble away.

These days, sunrooms can no longer be considered cold and uncomfortable to use, or ruinously expensive to maintain. Over the past ten to twenty years, new building materials and techniques have revived interest in them, leading to the current upsurge in popularity. Now, it seems, every homeowner wants to have a sunroom of their own.

One feature associated predominantly with the Edwardian style (although it can be used with others too) is the box gutter. This is a structural gutter used to join the sunroom to the house, in place of the more usual lead flashing. It is most commonly used for houses with low eaves, such as bungalows.

Nearly all modern sunrooms have gutters and rainwater vents built into the design. You should check these regularly to keep them free of obstructions. However, if you ever need to get onto the sunroom roof to access a gutter, never step directly on it, but use crawl boards to spread your weight.

A brand-new sunroom may take a little while to fit in with its environment. Building materials should always be matched as closely as possible with those of the original dwelling. However, bricks and mortar need to weather and blend in, particularly where old houses are concerned, and fresh landscaping may leave the surrounding area looking scarred for a time.

One solution is to plant flower beds around the exterior walls. These will quickly soften their outline, particularly if you train a creeper or two up the adjoining wall of the house. For a quick fix, simply arrange potted plants around the outside of the structure.

Newly laid paving also takes time to mellow. There are many attractive varieties of paving stone, including natural stone flags and their less expensive cement imitations. Terracotta tiles are very attractive, as are bricks, which can be arranged into herringbone patterns. Granite sets are slip-resistant; flints and cobblestones look good, though are hard to walk on. Using the same floor surface both inside and outside the sunroom creates a feeling of continuity between the two spaces.

Top tip: In winter, you are less likely to use outside doors leading to the garden. Additional rugs and furniture can therefore be arranged inside the sunroom to make the space more snug.

Sunrooms are not just for summer: They can be used all year round, even in the depths of winter, when they provide a snug refuge against the elements. For true year-round use, however, a more substantial construction is necessary than that required for a sunroom used only occasionally on warm, sunny days.

Double glazing is essential, as is a heavier roof structure. Polycarbonate roofing materials are supplied in different thicknesses, and the thicker they are, the better their insulating qualities. Efficient insulation makes the structure more environmentally sound, as it reduces fuel consumption—and, of course, saves you money on heating bills.

Sunrooms can be kept warm by electric fan heaters, and a wood- or coal-burning stove makes an attractive feature if you have the space for it. Most sunrooms, however, are heated by radiators plumbed into the house's central heating system. Numerous period styles are available, or alternatively the radiator may be boxed in behind a decorative grille.

Opposite: Candles create an elegant and romantic atmosphere for dining at night. However, remove them during the day: When temperatures rise, they are likely to melt.
Quantal Conservatory Roofing Systems

Right: Soft lighting, such as that provided by low-voltage halogen bulbs or standard lamps, is the best choice for sunrooms.
Quantal Conservatory Roofing Systems

At night as well as during the day, a sunroom provides a stylish space for dining, entertaining, or simply unwinding. A sunroom lit up at night has a warm and inviting atmosphere, and there is nothing more pleasant than sitting on a warm summer night, enjoying the sights and sounds of the garden while gazing at the stars overhead.

Lighting for sunrooms is an important consideration at the design stage. When planning your lighting, bear in mind that glass walls and ceilings act in a different way to solid interior walls: They allow light to escape rather than reflecting it. At the same time, however, they throw back harsh reflections if bright spotlights are used. Soft lighting works best, such as low-voltage halogen lighting, which can be installed along the roof beam or the frame to spotlight the room below. Freestanding standard lamps also work well. The most romantic lighting is provided by candles, but care should be taken to keep them away from flammable soft furnishings.

Unless you have no alternative, it is best not to place doors at the front of the sunroom, as this creates a corridor effect. Doors are better placed at the side of the structure, close to the main wall of the house, so as to minimize obstructions and maximize the amount of usable floor space.

The outside doors of the sunroom in the image shown opposite, which lead down to a garden, are offset from the internal doors that give access to the drawing room, on the raised ground floor level. The supporting walls are built of the same mellow stone as the period house itself, and the steps and wrought-iron railings echo those of the grand main entrance.

Incidentally, when you are drawing up plans for your sunroom, calculate its size on the basis of the internal floor space you require, allowing for the thickness of the walls. Most suppliers offer quotations based on external sizes, which can be significantly different. It's an easy mistake to make, and you could end up with less space than you imagined.

Chapter Six

Summerhouses, Pool Rooms, and Orangeries

Summerhouses

Opposite: This summerhouse-style sunroom was originally conceived as an addition to another part of the house, but the manufacturer suggested relocating it to make full use of the garden setting.
Tanglewood Conservatories, Denton, Maryland

Right: This octagonal structure sits apart from the main house, but is connected by a linking passageway. It functions as a self-contained garden room but is also part of the living space all year round.
Hampton Conservatories

A summerhouse is a small pavilion that stands away from the main house, usually in a sunny part of the garden. Certain specialist manufacturers produce sunrooms that echo the summerhouse style. These create a space that feels independent of the house, although in most cases the two remain physically connected.

Most traditional summerhouse designs are square or octagonal in shape, and built of wood with a shingle or tile roof. Most have windows on three sides and a solid back wall. All have double doors that open wide and, in most cases, can be folded back. Some are finished in rustic shades, such as green or brown, others are painted in more eye-catching colors, such as white or blue.

Summerhouses have long been popular with artists and writers, and are now also sometimes used as home offices. More commonly, however, they function as dining or entertainment areas, or simply as a quiet place to sit and read on a sunny day.

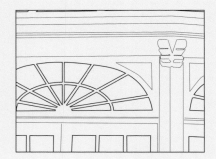

Some freestanding sunrooms are built in a traditional style, such as Victorian or Edwardian, while others have an octagonal shape, reminiscent of the summerhouse pavilion. In most cases, the structure remains connected to the main house, either by taking advantage of a corner position to install a set of double doors, or by means of a short glass passageway.

An interesting variation on the summerhouse theme is the patio roof enclosure. The example shown here was built for a client in Pennsylvania, who wanted to weatherproof a 20x24 ft flagstone patio, without spoiling her views of an acre of foliage and natural water features adjoining the house.

A steel subframe encased in timber supports the roof at eave level, with a steel corner post positioned behind a small tree, giving the impression that the glass roof is floating in mid-air. Protected from the elements, garden furniture can be left out on the patio, creating a light and airy extended living space.

Pool rooms

Right: The high gables
of this pool room allow light to
flood in. The pool-side area
accommodates sun loungers and
potted plants, while double doors
open onto the terrace.
Amdega Ltd

Opposite: This large structure
features a soaring, multi-faceted
polycarbonate roof, and has plenty
of pool-side space for furniture and
plant pots.
Ultraframe (UK) Ltd

If you have plenty of space and are not constrained by budget, why not consider a pool enclosure? A pool room makes an impressive feature, and in most cases can be used all year round. It is ideal for entertaining, or simply for keeping the kids amused through the long, hot summer days.

To accommodate a swimming pool of any size, the sunroom must of necessity be a large-span structure. Designs vary but, because of its large rectangular footprint and high roof, the orangery style is one of the most popular.

When designing a pool enclosure, include plenty of opening doors and windows for ventilation. Glazing should ideally extend all the way down to floor level: When you're swimming, your viewpoint is lower than normal, and solid walls mean you cannot see out. You may also want to incorporate a shower and changing room, a bathroom, and a bar or kitchen area into the building.

When drawing up your plans, be sure to leave plenty of room around the perimeter of the pool. Not only does this allow swimmers space to get in and out, it also makes a pleasant environment in which to sit and relax. Chairs and loungers, rugs, and pot plants help to create the right ambience.

This large pool room was built for a family in Perkasie, Pennsylvania. Its construction features a welded aluminium frame, with sliding glass doors surrounding the pool enclosure, and casement sash windows that allow cooling breezes to circulate on hot summer days.

Adjacent to the pool is a comfortable entertainment area furnished with cane chairs, which also includes a gas fireplace, a drinks bar, and a wine cooler. The whole pool room is kept warm by means of radiant floor heating, which means that the swimming pool can be used even in winter.

Right: This Georgian-style pool house was designed to blend in with the red brick and mortar of the existing house. The structure is framed with classically proportioned fluted columns. *Tanglewood Conservatories, Denton, Maryland*

Top tip: Pool rooms require a greater floor area than most normal sunrooms, including space for a changing area and a pool-side sitting area. You may also want an area for entertaining, a kitchen or bar, and probably also a bathroom. Pump equipment should be tucked away out of sight.

Left: This cantilevered lean-to pool room extends the space of the original house. Furniture is arranged in a comfortable sitting area, while the tiled area around the rool itself is easy to keep clean. Sliding doors lead to the garden. *Four Seasons Sunrooms*

Opposite: The luxurious interior features a circular spa-type plunge pool and contains exotic plants and citrus trees in pots, which complement the building's orangery-inspired design. *Tanglewood Conservatories, Denton, Maryland*

A pool room needs to accommodate pump and filtration equipment, heating, and perhaps also air-conditioning. Equipment of this sort invariably generates noise (at the least, an irritating hum), so it should be sited away from the main recreational area if possible. It can be hidden away in a separate service room or, in some cases, concealed underground.

Ventilation is of particular importance for pool rooms. Humidity and condensation may make the enclosure a good place for growing plants, but uncomfortable for its human occupants. There are a number of measures that can be taken to avoid the problem.

The structure should have plenty of opening doors and windows, and a high roof with vents, either manually operated or motorized. Heating both the air and the water helps to reduce condensation, as does a cover for when the pool is not in use (this also keeps out leaves and other floating debris). Double glazing helps to prevent unnecessary heat loss, making the pool room a space that can be enjoyed all year round.

Orangeries

The terms orangery and conservatory are sometimes used interchangeably. Both, however, refer back to the buildings' original function as places where exotic plants, especially citrus fruits, could be grown. In the Victorian heyday of botanical exploration, grand conservatories were showcases for exotic flora from around the world, and many still perform this function today.

Technically speaking, there are a number of important differences in the construction of an orangery and a conservatory. In general an orangery is architecturally stronger, with a deep profiled cornice running around the top of its glazed walls, and a box-like construction, which sometimes involves masonry. The extra strength is required to take the weight of the roof, which is normally cantilevered.

Internally, the box underside, or soffit, of the glazed roof runs all the way around the perimeter, and gives a greater feeling of enclosure than in a typical conservatory construction. The same is true of the detailing in the glazed walls, which typically feature wider frames incorporating pilaster columns.

Chapter Seven

Concept and Construction

Planning and design

Opposite and right:
The complex design for this upper-story sunroom in Oak Brook, Illinois, was drawn up by an architect. The owner wanted to incorporate a fireplace into the plans, so that the space could be enjoyed all year round.
Town and Country Conservatories

After your house itself, a sunroom is probably the single largest domestic investment you will make. Consider your choices carefully before rushing to build. Remember that a sunroom should be designed so that it looks like part of the original house, not an add-on. Consider the intended use of the room, its proportion to the principal building, its sun exposure, and the local climate.

Start off with the idea of "flow" between the different rooms, then consider the actual location of the sunroom, followed by its design and the choice of materials. Think about heating, lighting, and ventilation. Consider too what furniture, blinds, soft furnishings, and plants the sunroom may contain.

The new building should harmonize with the house, and be appropriate for the local style of architecture. It shouldn't be too big, and shouldn't encroach on neighbors' space. It should conform to local building regulations, and planning permission must be gained if necessary. It must also be safe, meaning that it won't collapse or create a fire hazard. A good supplier will be more than happy to advise you on all these issues.

Step-by-step construction

1. In this case study, the sunroom is to be added onto a typical new-build home in the United Kingdom. The exact construction procedure will vary from location to location, taking into account factors such as local architectural styles, soil type, and climate.

2. The first task is to excavate a trench for the footings, to a minimum depth of 18". Here, the excavation exposes an underground drainage pipe.

3. Steel mesh reinforcement is added to the concrete foundation to prevent the drainage pipe being crushed. Alternatively, concrete lintels could be used to bridge the pipe before the concrete is poured.

4. Concrete is poured into the trench to form the foundations. It should have a minimum depth of 6".

5. The concrete is floated to form a level building surface.

6. The inner leaf of the cavity wall is built up to the level of the floor.

7. Hardcore is laid to a minimum depth of 4" and compacted to form the base of the slab.

8. A layer of sand is poured over the hardcore to prevent any sharp stones puncturing the damp-proof membrane.

9. A damp-proof membrane is laid over the sand blinding and lapped onto the inner leaf of the brickwork. Additional floor insulation may be laid at this stage if required.

10. Concrete is laid to a depth of 4", to bring the slab up to the finished floor level.

11. The concrete is floated to a smooth, level surface, suitable for tiling. If you wish to lay a carpet, a screeded floor finish or self-levelling compound is usually added to the floor after the sunroom is erected.

Step-by-step construction

12. The outer leaf of the wall is built. In this case, artificial stone is used to match the brickwork of the house.

13. The inner leaf of the cavity wall is built to complete the basework.

14. A cavity tray is an optional installation, but is recommended if the site is exposed. The house wall is painted once the cavity trays and lead flashings have been installed.

15. A PVC-U external sill is fitted to the dwarf wall and erection of the side frames begins.

16. The structural aluminium eaves beam is fitted to the heads of the frames.

17. The aluminium glazing bars and ridge system, thermally clad with PVC-U, are assembled.

18. Polycarbonate glazing panels are installed to form the roof. Double-glazed units are a popular alternative.

19. The side frames are glazed once the roof frame is complete.

20. PVC-U internal cladding is fitted to the ventilated aluminium ridge. The cladding can be used to conceal electrical cables for lights or a ventilation fan.

21. The PVC-U internal fascia is clipped onto the eaves beam.

22. The sunroom is complete, ready for furnishing and use.
Pictures courtesy of Ultraframe (UK) Ltd

Frames

Left: PVC-U is hard-wearing, a good insulator, and needs little maintenance. White is the most common color, but dark brown variations are also available. *Quantal Conservatory Roofing Systems*

Opposite: This beautiful hardwood timber sunroom combines traditional design with modern features such as double-glazed window panels. *Hampton Conservatories*

Top tip: White is the traditional color for sunroom frames. Most prefabricated PVC-U units are white, though darker, wood-effect colors are also available. Timber frames require painting, and a wide choice of colors is available. Muted tones such as greens, grays, and light blues are among the most suitable.

The three most commonly used materials for sunroom frames are PVC-U, aluminium, and hardwood timber. Each has its advantages, but much depends on the style of your house and the extent of your budget. In general, go for the best you can afford, but be realistic in your expectations.

Timber is the most traditional material, and is particularly suited to period houses. It can be painted or stained almost any color. The downside is its higher cost, and the need for more regular maintenance.

PVC-U (or ultraviolet-resistant polyvinyl chlorate) is the cheapest of the three options and the most widely used. It needs little maintenance, and has excellent insulating qualities. It is mainly produced in white but also comes in darker colors, such as mahogany.

Aluminium costs more than PVC-U and does not insulate as efficiently, but it is stronger. Clad with a layer of PVC-U, it is often used in roof structures, where extra strength is required.

Glazing and roofing

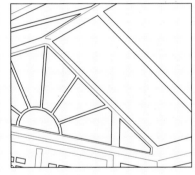

Sunroom glass is designed to be durable, and many types are tempered or laminated for extra strength. Glass wall panels or windows are most commonly supplied in the form of double-glazed sealed units. Typically, these are filled with inert air or gases such as argon, which improve their insulation properties.

Some glasses are tinted, or coated with a layer of microscopic metal particles, which helps to control the temperature and cut out harmful ultraviolet radiation. Low-emissivity (or Low E) coatings, used on brands such as Pilkington K, Celsius and Conservaglass, make the sunroom easier to keep warm in the winter, and prevent overheating in the summer. Thermally protected glass may cost more initially, but provides better insulation and will likely prove more durable than conventional materials in the long run.

Glass roofs are very stylish, allowing the light to flood in. On the other hand, they can be rather heavy and tend to be expensive. A cheaper and lighter option is polycarbonate, which is tough and provides good insulation. One drawback is its tendency to expand and contract in the heat, which causes it to creak and can eventually make it vulnerable to leaks.

Ventilation and heating

Opposite: A ceiling fan keeps the air circulating within the sunroom on hot days and is also an attractive decorative feature. *Ultraframe (UK) Ltd*

Right: This sunroom features a number of windows and small side vents that can be opened independently of one another. *Quantal Conservatory Roofing Systems*

Below: Here the job is done by low-profile skylight panels set into the roof of the structure. *British Conservatories Inc*

South- and west-facing sunrooms receive the most direct sunlight, and so need the most ventilation. Without it, on hot, sunny days temperatures quickly climb to uncomfortable levels. North- and east-facing sunrooms generally receive less sunlight. They are perfectly comfortable to use in the summer but are likely to require heating in the winter.

There are many different ventilation systems to choose from, ranging from simple side-opening windows to thermostat-controlled roof vents. These open and close automatically throughout the day, helping to maintain an even temperature and prevent an uncomfortable build-up of heat.

Hot air rises towards the roof ridge, and some designs incorporate trickle vent systems built into the frame that allow it to escape. The traditional ceiling fan is a popular option, and there are now also a number of air-conditioning systems on the market. The simplest way to ventilate a sunroom is to open windows and doors to allow air to circulate. Take care to secure them, however, to guard against possible wind damage.

Left: Automatic roof vents, controlled by heat-activated pistons, help to equalize the temperature throughout the day. *Ultraframe (UK) Ltd*

Opposite: Central heating and good ventilation help to avoid temperature extremes and the build-up of condensation. *Ultraframe (UK) Ltd*

The Victorians built elaborate heating systems powered by boilers, with pipes running under iron floor grilles. Nowadays the job is most often done by simply extending the domestic central heating system. An alternative is underfloor heating, using electric cables laid in sand. In winter, coal- or wood-fired cast-iron stoves create a cozy indoors atmosphere.

Condensation occurs when moist, warm air comes into contact with a cold surface, such as a glass wall. Most modern sunrooms incorporate double glazing, which is less susceptible to condensation than single panes. However, outside the summer months, condensation can still build up.

An abundance of plants is one factor that raises condensation levels. Newly built sunrooms can also take time to fully dry out— up to a year in some cases. If the problem is particularly bad, you may consider installing a dehumidifier. Usually, however, adequate heating and ventilation are all that is required. Manufacturers recommend opening vents with a combined area that amounts to at least 15 percent of the sunroom's floor area.

Details

Opposite left: This decorative gable, attached to an aluminium roof rafter, features the manufacturer's signature rose emblem.
British Conservatories Inc

Opposite right: Leaded lights, consisting of stained glass panels held in place by thin strips of lead, come in a wide variety of attractive designs, both custom-made and off-the-rack.
Tanglewood Conservatories, Denton, Maryland

Opposite right bottom: Dentil molding is a popular Victorian-style add-on that helps to create an attractive period appearance.
Ultraframe (UK) Ltd

Right: Roof crestings and finials come in a wide variety of shapes and styles, and can be made of wood, metal, or plastic.
Ultraframe (UK) Ltd

Architectural details are the finishing touches that give your sunroom its personality. For bespoke timber sunrooms at the top end of the market, they are sometimes made by hand. However, even factory-molded fittings can impart an enviable air of elegance. Manufacturers invariably have a number of different ranges from which you can choose, and some offer custom-made designs.

Decorative roof crestings, featuring a repeated, interlocking pattern, are found most frequently on Victorian- and Edwardian-style sunrooms. So too are finials, which provide a finishing touch at the apex of the roof. Finials can be round or pointed, and made of metal, treated wood, or plastic. Ornamental moldings are commonly placed at the point where the frame meets the roof, or incorporated into the frame itself.

Colored or patterned glass can be built into door panels, or incorporated into a clerestory level between the glass wall panels and the roof. Leaded light designs can be bought off-the-shelf, or designed to your own specifications. Sunrooms with a gable end usually have a pattern, such as a sunburst, built into their design.

Chapter Eight

Interior Design

Uses of sunrooms

Conservatories were originally designed to house plants. Although many sunrooms are still used for that purpose today, there are so many other uses to which they can be put. Adding an extra room to your house, and bridging the space between indoors and out, they infinitely extend your living possibilities.

The prime use of a sunroom is as an extra living room or sitting area. A good design will integrate the room into the rest of the house, with interior space flowing smoothly into the new, intermediate area where home and garden intersect. Living under glass literally opens up new horizons, creating a pleasing sensation of spaciousness.

Apart from simply sitting and relaxing, a sunroom can be used for entertaining friends and family, as a kitchen, as a play room for the kids, or as a home office. Imagine how much more relaxing it is to work in a light and airy sunroom, surrounded by plants, than in the traditional office environment.

Left and above: A Victorian sunroom adds an air of British charm and sophistication to this traditional American dining room.
Four Seasons Sunrooms

Opposite: The elegance of this dining area, with its plain pine furniture and wooden floor, lies in its very simplicity.
Renaissance Conservatories

A sunroom is particularly versatile as a dining area. In the morning it can be used as a sunny breakfast room; by night it becomes a place where you can enjoy the magical experience of dining under the stars. Provided it is properly heated and ventilated, meals can be taken there all year round.

A sunroom quickly becomes a hub for family life, particularly if it is adjoins, or is part of, the kitchen. In summer, sunroom doors can be opened onto the garden, and a terrace or patio area outside used to light a barbecue. A table can be set in the sunroom and, when it becomes chilly, guests can simply move back inside.

The interior décor of a dining area can be as simple or as elaborate as you like. Some people prefer a cozy atmosphere with blinds, curtains, and ornate dining tables and chairs; others favor a minimalist approach, with uncluttered surfaces and plain wooden furniture. The choice is entirely up to you.

Sunrooms allow time to relax and unwind from the stresses of modern living, affording you the opportunity for some quality time to yourself. Pursue your hobbies, or simply sit back and enjoy. Once you've got used to having one, you'll wonder how you ever managed to live without it.

One of the most luxurious ways to enjoy a sunroom is to install a hot tub or spa. What could be more relaxing than lying back in soothing warm water, watching the sun go down over the garden? Many different types of hot tub are available, and the interior of the sunroom can be designed around the style you choose.

Sports enthusiasts may create their own personal health club, installing home gymnasium equipment in their sunroom. Artists and craftspeople find them ideal as studios. And for gardeners, of course, they are the ideal place in which to pursue their hobby. A sunroom can be whatever you want it to be; the only limit is your imagination.

Flooring options

Opposite: The stone floor of this sunroom creates a cool and elegant living space and harmonizes with the natural landscape beyond.
K2 Conservatory Roof Systems

Center: Wooden laminate is an attractive alternative, though timber is prone to splitting after prolonged exposure to sunlight.
K2 Conservatory Roof Systems

Right: Floor tiles come in many different sizes and finishes, and may be plain or brightly decorated, and glazed or unglazed.
K2 Conservatory Roof Systems

Main picture: the stone floor sunroom creates a cool and elegant living space and harmonises with the natural landscape beyond

Far left: wooden laminate is an attractive alternative, though timber is prone to splitting after prolonged exposure to sunlight

Center and left: floor tiles come in many different sizes and finishes, and may be plain or brightly decorated

It is possible to carpet a sunroom floor if the space is to be used as an extension of a living room. However, if you intend to use it to its full potential as a garden room, more practical options are required. The most popular materials are tiles or stone paving, which are durable and easy to maintain.

Floor tiles, commonly either terracotta or ceramic, are available in many sizes, finishes, and textures. They may be plain or patterned, with many of the brightest designs originating from the Mediterranean region. They are also suitable for use in hallways. Stone flooring has a classical elegance. Slate, limestone, and sandstone are the most usual choices, while marble adds a touch of luxury. Stone and tile floors are wonderfully cool in summer, though in the winter they may benefit from a covering of rugs or grass matting.

Timber is a stylish alternative but be aware that, over time, exposure to strong sunlight may cause timber floors to warp and split. Laminated wooden surfaces may be treated to avoid this.

Blinds and shades

It may seem odd that a sunroom is fitted with blinds and shades to keep the sun out, but on hot days these are essential to maintain the temperature at a comfortable level, especially if the room is south-facing. At night, or if you are overlooked by neighbors, they can also afford a degree of privacy.

Various types of blinds and shades are available. Choosing the right one will depend on the style of your sunroom and the degree of protection you require. Fabric blinds are commonly used to cover roof and window panels. These can be pleated and operated by drawstrings (either manual or mechanized), or they can be in the form of roller-blinds.

Cane or bamboo blinds are a stylish choice, especially if you have cane or wicker furniture. Venetian blinds are sometimes used for wall panels. Pinoleum is a traditional material used for sunroom blinds. It is made of thinly sawn pieces of pinewood, sewn into strips, with a cloth edging. Pinoleum blinds are also sometimes known as Roman blinds.

Blinds prevent a sunroom becoming a hothouse, and allow it to be used in comfort even on the brightest of days. They can also help to protect furniture, carpets, and fabrics from the harmful effects of the sun, whose ultraviolet rays cause bleaching and fading over time.

Blinds should be considered as an integral part of the design right from the start. You need to work out the orientation of the sunroom and its exposure to the sun at different times of the day, and different times of year. When positioning blinds, you should avoid blocking roof vents. If you grow plants, be sure to train any climbing shoots away from cords and mechanisms.

Materials should be chosen to match the style of the sunroom and its intended use. For example, curtains might suit a sunroom if it functions primarily as a sitting or a dining room, but would look rather incongruous in a garden room.

The color palette

Opposite: The soft gray-green paint used on this timber conservatory matches the paintwork of the window frames and guttering of the house and helps it to blend into the garden. *Hampton Conservatories*

The interior décor of a sunroom is best coordinated to match the color of the external frame. With PVC-U and aluminium-framed sunrooms, the choice of color is limited largely to white and various dark brown finishes designed to resemble natural wood. Timber-framed sunrooms, however, can be painted, stained, or varnished in a wide variety of attractive colors.

White is the traditional color, derived from the white-lead paint used on Victorian greenhouses. Crisp white paintwork still works best in certain settings, and can help to brighten up dark corners if the sunroom is overshadowed by trees. In other settings, a less obtrusive color is more appropriate.

Most paint ranges comprise soft shades based on natural colors. These are designed to blend in with the garden setting and match the tones of traditional building materials, such as brick and stone. Creams and grays, buff and khaki, and various shades of green are all popular. So too are soft gray-blues that match the color of the sky. The interior may be painted in the same color, or in a complementary shade.

Furniture

Left: Glass-topped tables with a cane or bamboo frame are light and informal and, if required, can be covered over with a table cloth at meal times.
Quantal Conservatory Roofing Systems

Opposite: Stylish garden furniture made of wicker, cane, or rattan blurs the boundary between house and garden and makes the sunroom a comfortable place in which to relax.
Amdega Ltd

Sunrooms occupy a unique space between house and garden, and stylish garden furniture adds immensely to their appeal. The most popular types of sunroom furniture are made from materials such as wicker, cane, and rattan. Wicker is formed from willow shoots, while rattan and cane are produced largely in the Far East.

The informal style of these materials is perfectly suited to outdoor living. They are comfortable to use, and tough enough to withstand high levels of sunlight and humidity. As well as for chairs and loungers, they are commonly used for tables, which sometimes also have a glass top.

Alternatively, seats can be made of wood or wrought iron, with tie-on cushions. Ornate Victorian-style benches and tables made of wrought iron are very elegant and can double up as outdoor garden furniture in the summer months.

Unless a sunroom is used as a dining or sitting room, polished wooden furniture is usually best avoided. It looks rather formal, and is vulnerable to both bright sunlight and damp. If this is your preferred style, however, careful positioning of blinds can help to protect wooden surfaces.

Chapter Nine

Plants and Gardens

The indoor garden

Sunrooms evolved originally as plant houses, and they are still the perfect environment in which to grow a wide variety of plants. Conservatory gardening is not especially difficult. With a little basic care and attention, you can enjoy a luxuriant indoor garden all year round, even in the depths of winter.

The brief for this Georgian-style conservatory in North Yorkshire was to create an extra living room that would link the house with the garden. The structure itself is light and airy, and generously proportioned. The use of the same paving slabs both inside and out softens the division between the two and allows the living area to extend to the terrace outside. Inside, the owners have trained a luxuriant passionflower vine over the roof supports, while outside they have positioned colourful plants in terracotta plants. A selection of comfortable wicker furniture and tasteful soft furnishings completes the picture.

Plants and gardens

Top tip: Planting flower beds immediately outside a conservatory will soften its outlines and help it to blend in with the garden. Filling the interior with plants in pots will further blur the distinction. Scented plants such as lavender and honeysuckle will add to the enjoyment of the space in summer.

Right: Filled with plants on the inside and surrounded by foliage outside, this conservatory is a point where house and garden meet. *Amdega Ltd*

In the summer months, a conservatory provides a transitional space between indoors and out, perfect for dining, entertaining, or simply relaxing. Doors can be opened wide onto the terrace or garden, extending the available living space and giving clear views of the garden from inside the house.

When planting is mature, a conservatory can literally become part of the garden. In the example shown here, the structure is surrounded by trees and luxuriant planting while the inside is filled with climbing plants. Large, plain glazing panels blur the distinction between inside and out, while the green-painted frame allows the structure to blend into its surroundings.

Double doors lead outside to a small gravelled area, surrounded by scented border plants. On the lawn sits a pair of weathered wooden sun loungers. Garden furniture made of wood, steel, or galvanized iron, and mosaic tile tables, can be left outside all year round. Light wicker or plastic furniture can be moved in and out as required.

Plants suitable for sunrooms

Many different types of plant can be cultivated in a conservatory. Species native to the warmer zones of the tropics and the Mediterranean do well under glass, even in the temperate climates of northern Europe and the United States. They will survive through the cold winter months and reward the indoor gardener with pretty blooms and delicious scents all year round.

Among the most popular sunroom species are flowering plants such as hibiscus, camellias, and morning glory; scented climbers such as jasmine and bougainvillaea; and exotic blooms such as lilies and orchids. The cultivation of ornamental ferns dates back to Victorian times, and there are many species to choose from, including spectacular tree ferns.

Many types of fruiting plant can also be grown. Citrus trees (orange, lemon, and grapefruit), banana plants, and grapevines are all species that flourish under glass. Olive trees and tomatoes can be grown in pots. If your sunroom is adjacent to a kitchen, try growing herbs such as chives, mint, and coriander. Pot plants can be rotated throughout the year as plants mature.

The orientation of a conservatory affects the types of plant that can be grown. A shaded north-facing conservatory, for instance, has a relatively even temperature throughout the year, which encourages the growth of foliage. This is good for ornamental plants such as ferns and ivies. A south-facing conservatory is much hotter, encouraging the growth of flowering plants and blossom.

The main concern is to balance the needs of plants with the needs of people. It is unrealistic to cultivate exotic species that demand heat and high humidity. Such conditions are difficult to maintain and make the sunroom uncomfortable as a living space.

Don't let plants get too large—they should be regularly pruned. Climbing plants can grow remarkably quickly, and care should be taken to train them away from blinds and roof vents. Although deciduous plants keep their leaves longer under glass, many (such as grapevines) still shed them in winter. For this reason, evergreens—for example, jasmine—may be a better choice.

Plants should be regularly watered and kept moist. In most sunrooms, it doesn't matter if you splash a little water on the floor.

Planters and statues

Top tip: Architectural salvage centers are great hunting grounds for statues and fountains. Many of these items may be valuable antiques, rescued from grand old houses that have been demolished or modernized. A more economical option is to visit your local garden center. Most modern reproduction items, in stone or fiberglass, are a fraction of the cost.

Plant beds can be created inside a conservatory, but most plants tend to be grown in pots. Pots have the advantage that they can be moved around to suit the layout of the room, or to create different moods. They also allow plants to be rotated as they bloom at different times of the year, or moved outside onto a terrace in the summer, as was the practice with the original orangeries.

There are many types of containers. In classic orangery style, citrus trees are often grown in square wooden tubs, painted white or green. When it comes to pots, there is a vast choice of styles and sizes, in terracotta and ceramics.

Hanging baskets make an attractive feature, suspended from roof supports. They are ideal for ornamental ferns and ivies. Jardinieres are wire structures that hold a number of different plant pots, allowing an impressive display to be created.

For a truly ornamental touch, consider placing a statue or two in your indoor garden. The Victorians were fond of nymphs and shepherds, nudes, and classical figures, sculpted in marble or lead, and sometimes created elaborate grottoes complete with running water. Salvage centers and garden suppliers will provide modern inspiration.

Landscaping

Integrating the sunroom into its surroundings is an essential part of the design and construction process. Sometimes this involves a certain amount of landscaping, where earth has to be either dug out, or banked up, to provide a smooth transition to the garden. In some cases, a raised floor can be built on joists, and the space underneath used as storage space for garden tools or furniture.

A patio, or an area covered with gravel, directly outside the sunroom makes a pleasant place to sit on a warm day. For larger houses, a terrace with steps leading down to the garden makes an impressive feature. Double doors can be folded back in summer and the terrace used for entertaining.

Planting borders immediately outside the sunroom with fragrant plants, such as lavender, means that on warm summer evenings you can sit inside and enjoy the scents wafting in on the breeze. Even in towns, where space may be limited, the same result can be achieved by cultivating plants in pots and placing them on steps or in the back yard. This will also help to create the impression that the sunroom is an integral part of its surroundings.

Choosing the Right Builder

Finding a supplier

Opposite: The addition of a sunroom will completely transform the appearance of your house and the way it relates to its surroundings. *Ultraframe (UK) Ltd*

Right: Before contacting suppliers, establish what kind of sunroom you want, and how it will fit into the space available. *Quantal Conservatory Roofing Systems*

Buying a sunroom is a major decision, ranking in terms with moving or buying a new car. It is not something to be entered into lightly. You need to be sure that the supplier you choose will provide you with the product you want, at the right price, and within a reasonable timescale.

There are many places to look for sunroom suppliers—the list of manufacturers at the back of this book is a good start, and homes and interiors magazines, local newspapers, and the Internet are all also good sources. If you have friends or family, or neighbors or work colleagues, who have a sunroom, ask them who built it, and whether they would recommend them.

Before approaching companies, however, decide what sort of sunroom you want, and how you plan to use it throughout the year. Timber frames may look the most elegant, but if you want a low-cost and easy-to-maintain sunroom, aluminium or PVC-U may be a wiser choice. Establish how much space is available for construction, and how the sunroom will connect with the house. Armed with a rough outline of your requirements, you will be better equipped to start obtaining quotes.

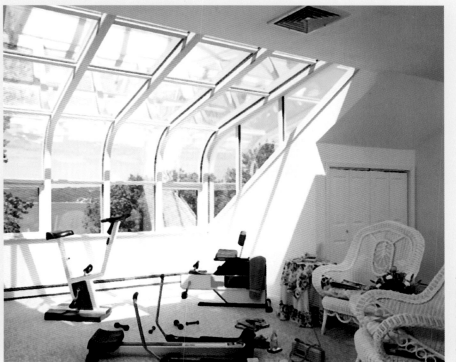

Left: Get a number of quotes from different companies, and always be sure to check exactly what is included in the price. This relatively simple attic bump-out is used as a home gymnasium. *Four Season Sunrooms*

Opposite: For particularly large projects or specialist designs, a company will generally draw up blueprint plans to your own specifications, however unusual. *Renaissance Conservatories*

Top tip: Some sunroom suppliers are local to a particular area and specialize in a particular style of sunroom; others are national in scope and offer a wide range of styles. These days, nearly all have websites detailing their products and services, so an internet search is a good way to start getting a feel for the vast range of options available.

Once you have identified companies supplying the type of sunroom that you want, you will most likely be visited in your home by a salesperson who will measure the proposed space, take you through a list of design options, and give you a quotation for the completed job.

The salesperson may well use a laptop computer running design software similar to that featured on the enclosed DVD. This allows them to attach designs to a digital photo of your house, so you can see how different options might look in reality.

Always be sure to establish exactly what is included in the quoted price. Items such as argon-filled double-glazing units, thermal glass, and decorative leaded lights, for example, usually all cost extra. A glass roof is more expensive than a polycarbonate one. Be sure also to ask about warranties.

It's wise to get a number of different quotes, but don't necessarily go for the cheapest. Buy the best you can afford, from a company you feel you can trust.

Left: Some suppliers take responsibility for construction of the sunroom themselves, but in many cases the work is sub-contracted out to building firms. *Four Seasons Sunrooms*

Opposite: With confidence in your choice of builder, you can look forward to sitting back and relaxing in your new sunroom. *Renaissance Conservatories*

Be sure to establish how the company proposes to carry out the work. Some companies undertake the entire project themselves, from beginning to end. Others may sub-contract out the building work to a partner company or to a building contractor. Some of these in turn may sub-contract out specialist tasks such as electrical wiring or plumbing in radiators.

In other cases, the manufacturer may simply supply the sunroom in kit form. You may then decide to assemble it yourself, or hire an independent builder.

Whoever you choose to work on the project, it is vital that they are reliable and trustworthy. Ask yourself whether you feel you can trust the person in your home, even when you're not around. Find out whether they propose to clear up any mess at the end of each working day.

Your relationship with your builder is critical, and you must feel comfortable with them, even if the work itself runs into problems. Once the job has started, it is very difficult to go back on your decision, so take your time and select well.

Resources

Manufacturers and suppliers

Admiral Sunroom Corp.
2120 California Avenue
Corona, CA 92881 USA
tel: +1 909 549 9810
fax: +1 909 549 9811
website: www.admiralsunrooms.com

Amdega Ltd
Faverdale, Darlington
Co. Durham DL3 0PW UK
tel: +44 (0)800 591523
email: info@amdega.co.uk
website: www.amdega.com

Canada and USA:
tel: +1 800 449 7348

Republic of Ireland, Europe, and Asia:
tel: +44 (0)1325 468522

British Conservatories Inc
5004 Mt Vernon Avenue
Temple, PA 19560 USA
tel: +1 610 939 8969
fax: +1 610 939 9464
email: britishrose@comcast.net
website: www.britishrose.com

**Burgin Conservatory Design
& Furnishings**
21 Bushley Wood Road
Dore, Sheffield S17 3QA UK
tel: +44 (0) 114 235 1665
fax: +44 (0) 114 235 2356
email: gaburgin@netcomuk.co.uk

Canterbury Conservatories Ltd
Airport Technical Center
136 West 64th Street
Holland, MI 49423 USA
tel: +1 616 394 0303
fax: +1 616 394 3004
email: inquiry@canterburyconservatory.com
website: www.canterburyconservatory.com

Classic Conservatories
website: www.classicconservatories.com

Conservatory Supplies Ltd
The Conservatory Centre
Leigh Sinton Road, Malvern
Worcestershire WR14 1JP UK
tel: +44 (0)1684 575588
email: sales@CSLtd.net
website: www.CSLtd.net

Creative Structures Conservatories
1770 Main Street
Hellertown, PA 18055 USA
tel: +1 800 873 3966
website: www.creativeconservatories.com

Four Seasons Solar Products LLC
5005 Veterans Memorial Highway
Holbrook, New York 11741-4507 USA
tel: +1 631 563 4000/+1 800 368 7732
fax: +1 631 563 4010
website: www.FourSeasonsSunrooms.com

Garden Under Glass
11 Vanderbilt Parkway
Dix Hills, New York 11746 USA
tel: +1 631 424 5997
website: www.gardenunderglass.com

Hampton Conservatories
218 Ballybogey Road
Portrush, County Antrim
N. Ireland BT56 8NE UK
tel (Belfast): +44 (0)28 7082 4100
tel (Dublin): +353 (0)1 8551512
tel (New York): +1 631 271 4177
email: sales@hamptonconservatories.uk.com
website: www. hamptonconservatories.uk.com

Showroom:
Wilson's Yard
123 Hillsborough Road
Dromore, County Down BT25 1QW UK

K2 Conservatory Roof Systems
Burnden Works, Burnden Road
Bolton, Lancashire BL3 2RB UK
tel: +44 (0)1204 554554
fax: +44 (0)1204 554577
email: enquiry@K2Conservatories.com
website: www. K2Conservatories.com

Posh Windows and Conservatories
website: www.posh.co.uk

Quantal Conservatory Roofing Systems
Units 9/10, International House
Battle Road, Heathfield Industrial Estate
Newton Abbott, Devon TQ12 6RY UK
tel: +44 (0)1626 832355
website: www.quantal.co.uk

Renaissance Conservatories
132 Ashmore Drive
Leola, PA 17540 USA
tel: +1 800 882 4657
fax: +1 717 661 7727
website: www.renaissance-online.com

Sundance Supply
Olga, WA USA
website: www.sundancesupply.com

SunPorch Structures, Inc.
495 Post Road East
Westport, CT 06880 USA
tel: +1 203-454-0040 (ext. 10)/+1 800-221-2550
fax: +1 203-454-0020
email: info@sunporch.com
website: www.sunporch.com

Tanglewood Conservatories Ltd
15 Engerman Avenue
Denton, MD 21629 USA
tel: +1 410 479 4700
website: www.tanglewoodconservatories.com

Town and Country
Horningtoft
Dereham, Norfolk NR20 5DJ UK
tel: +44 (0)1328 700565
fax: +44 (0)1328 700015
email: info@masterworksinglass.com
website: www.masterworksinglass.com

North America:
1475 West Foster Ave.
Chicago, IL 60640 USA
tel: +1 773 506 8000
fax: +1 773 506 8815
website: www.town-country.net

Tull & Darch
14/15 Ordnance Court
Ackworth Road, Hilsea
Portsmouth PO3 5RX UK
tel: +44 (0)1794 340946
fax: +44 (0)1794 342133
email: info@tullndarch.com
website: www.tullndarch.com

Ultraframe
Enterprise Works
Salthill Road, Clitheroe
Lancashire BB7 1PE UK
tel: +44 (0)1200 452331
fax: +44 (0)1200 414646
website: www.ultraframe.com

Versatile Conservatory Roof Systems
Units 1-11, Prince of Wales Industrial Estate
Abercarn, Gwent NP11 5AR UK
tel: +44 (0)1495 247233
fax: +44 (0)1495 240660
email: sales@versatileltd.co.uk

Wedgwood Conservatories
81 Northfield Avenue
West Orange, NJ 07052 USA
tel: +1 800 892 0551
fax: +1 952 892 1305
website: www.wedgwoodconservatories.com

Conservatory design software

Windowlink Ltd
Minety, Malmesbury
Wiltshire, SN16 9QY UK
tel: +44 (0)870 770 1640/+44 (0)800 028 2160
fax: +44 (0)870 770 2960
email: sales@windowlink.com
website: www.windowlink.com

Other useful addresses

Conservatories Online
website: www.conservatoriesonline.com
Practical construction advice and online buyer's guide.

The Crystal Palace Foundation and Crystal Palace Museum
Anerley Hill, London SE19 2BA UK
tel: +44 (0)7889 338812
website: www.crystalpalacefoundation.org.uk

The Eden Project
Bodelva
St Austell, Cornwall PL24 2SG UK
tel: +44 (0)1726 811911
website: www.edenproject.com

Endless Pools
website: www.endlesspools.com
Aquatic exercise pools.

Photo Credits

Amdega Ltd.

British Conservatories Inc

Canterbury Conservatories Ltd.

Four Seasons Solar Products

Hampton Conservatories

K2 Conservatory Roof Systems

Quantal Conservatory Roofing Systems

Renaissance Conservatories

SunPorch Structures, Inc.

Tanglewood Conservatories Ltd

Town and Country Conservatories

Tull & Darch

Ultraframe (UK) Ltd

Glossary

Box gutter A structural gutter used to attach a sunroom to a building, often where height is limited (for example, a single-story bungalow). Used most commonly with Edwardian-style sunrooms.

Bump-out Small sun space that extends an interior room, without being a stand-alone structure and not necessarily having its own doors to the outside.

Clerestory An extra level of glazing inserted between the top of a glazed wall and the roof. Used to add height and increase light penetration, also frequently features decoration such as colored glass. Sometimes referred to as a transom light.

Cornerfill A sunroom filling a corner space created by the angle of two house walls.

Cresting Decorative motif running along the ridge of a sunroom roof. There are many different types, based on a variety of architectural styles. Can be made of wood, plastic, or aluminium and can be part of the structure, or simply clipped on to the frame.

Dentil molding One of many different types of decorative molding for sunroom frames, and one of the most popular. It features a repeated pattern of small square ridges, inspired by classical Greek and Roman architecture.

Dwarf wall Sometimes called a knee wall, this serves as the foundation for the sunroom superstructure. Normally built as a cavity wall, for extra insulation, using building materials that match the style of the house.

Edwardian Popular style of sunroom, based on the architecture of the British Edwardian era. Characterized by a rectangular footprint, and normally with a hipped roof.

Finial A decorative feature fitted at the apex of a roof. Can be round, pointed or elaborately molded, and made of wood, plastic, or aluminium.

Flashing Lead sheeting attached at the point where the sunroom structure joins the house wall, to keep water out.

Georgian Popular style of sunroom, based on the architecture of the British Georgian era. Characterized by a rectangular footprint with a gable end, which usually incorporates a decorated glazing pattern section.

Glazing bar Structural element used to support glazing panels forming the roof of the sunroom.

Hipped roof Triangular roof section sloping up towards the ridge, most often associated with Edwardian-style sunrooms.

Knee wall See dwarf wall.

Lantern Additional raised roof section. Used for decoration and to admit more light.

Lean-to Simplest style of sunroom, and one of the most popular.

Ogee An S-shaped decorative molding.

Orangery The prototype for the modern sunroom. Originating in the eighteenth century, they were built with masonry walls and large sash windows. The style is still popular today for larger sunrooms, particularly pool enclosures.

Pilaster Rectangular column forming part of a wall, used as an ornamental molding.

Sash window Window with an opening lower half attached to a cord. Popular in the Georgian era, and still the model for many types of sunroom glazing today.

Sill Shelf created by the dwarf wall, running round the interior of a sunroom. Commonly used for displaying potted plants and ornaments.

Soffit Underside of a roof surface, usually in an orangery.

Snow loading The pressure exerted on a sunroom roof by heavy deposits of snow. Roofing systems are stringently tested to meet safety requirements, particularly in the United States.

Victorian Popular style of sunroom, based on the architecture of the British Victorian era. Characterized by a ridge running at 90 degrees to the main house and a bell-shaped front section.

About the Author

David Wilson is a freelance journalist and author. Born in West Wales in 1961, he studied languages at Oxford and subsequently spent time living and working in France, Italy, and Japan. Travel remains a passion. He is also a keen photographer, and began writing for the UK photographic press in 1985. He now works for a wide variety of publications, both in the UK and internationally, covering subjects that range from the visual arts to international business and development.

He has published three previous books, all on practical aspects of photography, with visual arts publisher RotoVision. They are *The Better Picture Guide to Portraits*, *Commercial Photo Series: Children*; and *Professional Photography: Photographing Buildings*.

Acknowledgments

Thanks are due first and foremost to Angie Patchell, who came up with the idea for the book and provided support and guidance throughout. A big thank you also to Dan Moscrop, who designed the book, produced the illustrations, and also took the flower photographs that grace the opening pages of each chapter.

This project would not, of course, have been possible without the support and assistance of the many companies in the conservatory industry who took the time to supply photographs and share their valuable expertise. Special thanks go to Iain McInnes at K2 for checking technical content, Mark Hanson at Ultraframe for supplying the step-by-step construction guide, and John Guy at Tull & Darch for the line drawings. Special thanks also to Giles Hayhurst and Barrie Ryan at Windowlink for supplying the content of the attached CD. However, the assistance of all who contributed is most gratefully acknowledged.